THE OFFICE

A SURVIVAL GUIDE

MARTIN BAXENDALE

DISCLAIMER: The author and publisher wish to make it crystal clear that they accept no (that's <u>no</u>) responsibility for any demotion, dismissal, loss of company benefits, garroting by boss, lynching by co-workers, or any other repercussions (including sniggering and pointing) that may result from anyone being daft enough to take any of the ludicrous advice in this book too seriously.

Having said that, we also guarantee (for the purposes of selling lots of books and making ourselves piles of money) that you will be C.E.O. or Chairman of a multinational company within weeks or even days of reading this incredible self-help manual.

CONTENTS

FOREWORD

A personal message from Martin Baxendale:

"Having worked in various offices over the years, I thought I'd managed to escape the daily routine of office life when I started working as a writer and cartoonist from home.

Wrong!! I'm still stuck in an office all day, still chained to a desk, and still have a slave-driving <u>boss</u> constantly on my back...."

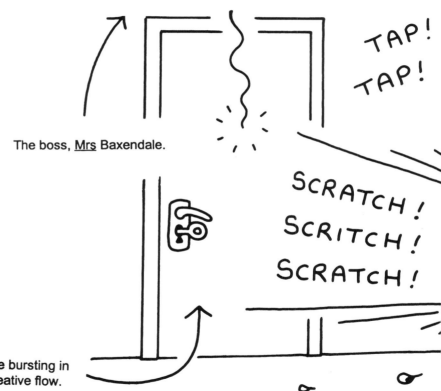

The boss, <u>Mrs</u> Baxendale.

Door locked, to stop Mrs Baxendale bursting in and interrupting Mr Baxendale's creative flow.

A personal message from <u>Mrs</u> Baxendale:

"What he doesn't know is that I'm actually down at the local bistro having a long boozy lunch, followed by a sauna and massage at the health and beauty club."

KEEP WORKING, YOU LAZY SOD! WE'VE GOT BILLS TO PAY!

Door bolted to stop Mr Baxendale getting out.

OFFICE

YES DEAR!

Tape of Mrs Baxendale shouting encouraging remarks to Mr Baxendale through office door at regular intervals.

INTRODUCTION

Long hours, boring daily routines, endless paperwork, slave-driving bosses, people borrowing your stapler without asking — just some of the many annoying problems that can plague the life of any office worker.

But don't worry; the following pages are stuffed with valuable tips and hints to help you survive the daily grind and return home with your sanity intact, no-one murdered, and your stapler safely tucked up in your desk drawer where it belongs.

BASIC OFFICE COMPONENTS AND THEIR USES

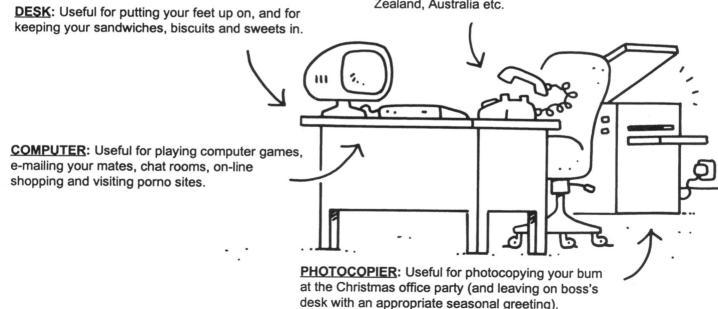

TELEPHONE: Useful for calling friends and long natters with relatives who've emigrated to New Zealand, Australia etc.

DESK: Useful for putting your feet up on, and for keeping your sandwiches, biscuits and sweets in.

COMPUTER: Useful for playing computer games, e-mailing your mates, chat rooms, on-line shopping and visiting porno sites.

PHOTOCOPIER: Useful for photocopying your bum at the Christmas office party (and leaving on boss's desk with an appropriate seasonal greeting).

FILING CABINET: Useful for hiding your office booze in (filing your booze alphabetically will also help you to lay hands on exactly the bottle you fancy when you need to take the edge off a particularly bad day - e.g. 'V' for vodka, 'S' for scotch, 'M' for metal polish).

BOSS: Useful for....er....um....well, not a lot, generally speaking.

AAARGH!!!

GLUG!

LEAP!

WATER COOLER: Useful for adding laxatives and/or hallucinogenic drugs to when your co-workers have really pissed you off (or just to relieve the boredom and have a bit of fun).

WINDOW: Useful for when you can't take it any longer.

9

THE BOSS

If you've got a good boss you're one of the lucky ones, because as we all know, there are some real bastards out there – nasty, tiny-minded, bullying slave-drivers who love to make their workers' lives a misery. Not _my_ boss of course; Mrs Baxendale (see foreword) couldn't be more considerate, caring and helpful..........or so she tells me.

BASIC FEATURES OF A <u>GOOD</u> BOSS.

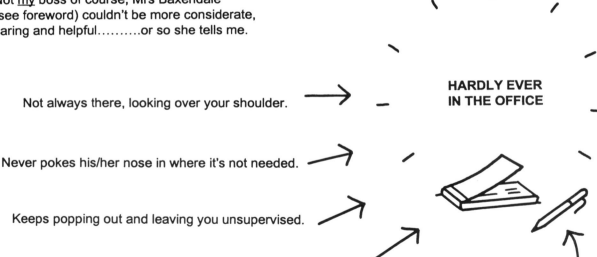

HARDLY EVER
IN THE OFFICE

Not always there, looking over your shoulder.

Never pokes his/her nose in where it's not needed.

Keeps popping out and leaving you unsupervised.

Constantly leaves cheque book behind.

Has signature that's dead easy to forge.

BASIC FEATURES OF A **BAD** BOSS.

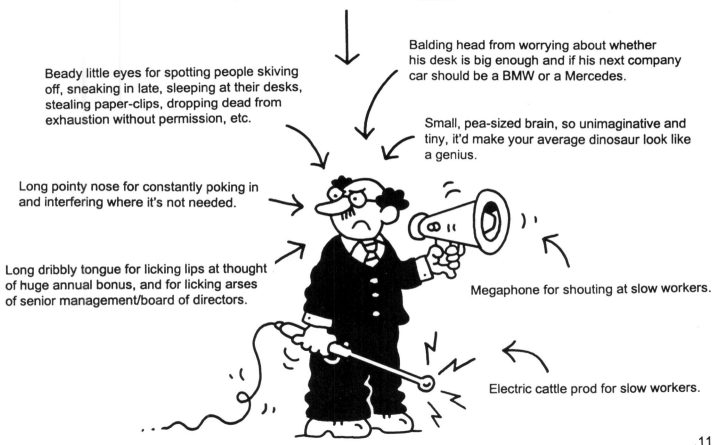

Beady little eyes for spotting people skiving off, sneaking in late, sleeping at their desks, stealing paper-clips, dropping dead from exhaustion without permission, etc.

Balding head from worrying about whether his desk is big enough and if his next company car should be a BMW or a Mercedes.

Small, pea-sized brain, so unimaginative and tiny, it'd make your average dinosaur look like a genius.

Long pointy nose for constantly poking in and interfering where it's not needed.

Long dribbly tongue for licking lips at thought of huge annual bonus, and for licking arses of senior management/board of directors.

Megaphone for shouting at slow workers.

Electric cattle prod for slow workers.

BOSS EARLY-WARNING SYSTEM.

Something on these lines is useful if you don't want your boss to keep catching you playing computer games, making private phone calls, sleeping at your desk, etc. when you should be working.

Of course, even all this may be no use if your boss is very, very sneaky and clever at creeping up on you (or has seen too many Tom Cruise action films).

Walking across ceiling wearing high-tech suction-shoes.

Pressure pads under carpet all around your desk set off warning light when stepped on.

Infra-red motion sensors covering all approaches to your desk.

Sensitive heat-detectors set off warning light if they pick up even slight rise in air temperature from body heat of another person approaching your desk.

HIDING FROM THE BOSS.

Whether your boss is looking for you to give you a bollocking, dump extra work onto you or just generally make your life miserable, it's handy to have some imaginative hiding places (other than the obvious places where he's bound to look, like the office toilets, or under your desk).

Amongst office plants (always a good idea to build up a large collection of these, as it not only gives you somewhere to hide but, in a large enough plantation, somewhere to sling a hammock for a crafty snooze).

Inside coffee machine.

Inside dummy filing cabinet (no drawers).

COPING WITH A BAD BOSS.

If you find yourself stuck with a really shitty, nasty, bullying boss, don't just get mad - get even!

There are many ways to get your own back on a bullying, slave-driving boss, and most are also great fun.

Voodoo doll of boss.

Hide piece of fish in ventilator/heating vent. As it starts to rot, will stink out boss's office with vile stench.

Catch big fat bluebottle flies (the really annoying loud, fast-flying kind) at home and release into boss's office first thing every morning before he comes in (eventually will find the rotting fish and start to breed in large numbers).

BUZZZ!

BUZZZ!

MUNCH!
CHOMP!

Inject boss's expensive leather executive chair with milk. Disgusting vomit-like stink will gradually develop as it goes off.

Tape under boss's big expensive executive desk a piece of wood infested with wood-devouring pests like woodworm, termites, deathwatch beetle or (best of all if you can get them) giant Bolivian wood weevils, to eat his precious desk away from under him.

TICK!
TOCK!

Annoying sound of deathwatch beetle.

HOW TO AVOID GETTING SACKED.

The best way to do this is always to have something on your boss that you can use to ensure you keep your job no matter how many times you're caught coming in late, skiving off, sleeping at your desk, etc.

Office parties, for example, can provide excellent opportunities to entrap your boss in the kind of situations that should ensure you keep your job for life (and help when negotiating salary increases).

OI! STOP LOOKING DOWN MY TOP!!

DO YOUR FUNNY IMPERSONATION OF THE COMPANY CHAIRMAN!

WHIRRR!

TUG!

Hidden video camera.

Boss's drink spiked with huge amounts of vodka.

COPING WITH CO-WORKERS

THE ANNOYING CO-WORKER.

A co-worker with an annoying habit (tuneless whistling, constant humming, finger-tapping etc) can quickly drive you to distraction if you don't put a stop to it.

An electric stun-gun comes in handy here, discreetly wired to needle-probes in the seat of the co-worker's chair. With the stun-gun set to 'low', you can administer appropriate aversion-therapy shocks to his or her bottom whenever the annoying behaviour occurs (blame static from the carpet if they get suspicious).

THE "BORROWER" CO-WORKER.

Equally annoying is co-workers who habitually "borrow" stuff from your desk (pens, stapler, calculator, etc) and never put it back, or who help themselves to your stash of chocolate biscuits, sweets, etc when they think you're not looking.

You can fix this with a strong spring fitted to the back of your desk drawer, that snaps the drawer shut with digit-denting force just as the pilfering co-worker lets go of the handle and puts his or her fingers inside to get at your goodies.

THE SMELLY OR INFECTIOUS CO-WORKER.

There's nothing worse (especially in hot weather) than having to share an office with a revoltingly smelly co-worker; whether it's someone who has pongy feet and/or smelly armpits, farts all the time, chain-smokes constantly despite your objections, or insists on wearing eye-wateringly powerful aftershave or chokingly pungent perfume.

Just as bad is the inconsiderate co-worker who insists on coming in to work even though they have a ghastly cold or flu, and sneezing and coughing all over you until you've got it too.

Make smelly and/or infectious co-worker wear chemical warfare style all-body isolation hood with extractor fan to outside wall or window, or (better still) vent the smelly and infectious fumes into boss's office.

COUGH!

SNEEZE!

FART!

SLEEPING AT YOUR DESK.

This 'Wide Awake' (®™) disguise has allowed me to spend many lazy hours happily snoozing at my desk instead of working, without getting found out by the eagle-eyed <u>Mrs</u> Baxendale (who really knows how to use an electric cattle prod if she catches you not working flat-out). Trust me, it'll fool <u>your</u> boss too.

Cut ping-pong ball in half and paint to look like wide-awake eyeballs, then sellotape over real eyes before nodding off to sleep. Note: make pin-holes in middle of painted eyes, to see through; so when you wake up you don't think you've gone blind, panic and scream in terror, which can really give the game away (that's how I was nearly caught the first time!)

Cotton-wool plugs in nostrils to dampen-down any snoring noises.

Stops you nodding and falling forward across desk.

Discreet wrist-bands with springs on suckers attached to desk top, make your hands bounce around over keyboard, calculator, paperwork, etc., as if working.

19

PRETENDING TO BE BUSY.

An essential office skill if you don't want your boss constantly dumping more and more work onto you, eating into your valuable magazine-perusing, book-reading, crossword-solving and general daydreaming time.

Take cover off computer manual and tape over cover of latest must-read bestseller novel. While reading novel, occasionally tap computer keys, glare at screen and swear loudly as if struggling with computer problem.

Staple your favourite magazine or crossword puzzle inside office file with boring title (e.g. VAT receipts) so no-one is likely to poke their nose in. While reading magazine or doing crossword puzzle, occasionally tap calculator keys, shake head and groan loudly.

Water sprayer. Regularly spray water onto forehead and under armpits, to give impression that you're working up a real sweat.

Giant economy-size aspirin jar filled with mints. Keep stuffing your mouth, to give the impression of splitting headache due to heavy workload.

CALLING IN "SICK".

If you're phoning the office from home pretending to be sick so you can skive off for the day, it's important to make it sound realistic to your boss on the other end.

The secret of success, as with any dramatic production, is a believable script, good acting and realistic special effects.

I'M EXPLODING AT BOTH ENDS.... OH, NO! MY NICE NEW CARPET... RUINED!!

DEAR GOD! I DON'T WANT YOU ANYWHERE NEAR THE OFFICE IN THAT STATE!

SPLLRRP!

SPLLRRP!

SPLLRRP!

SPLLRRP!

Violent projectile-vomiting and diarrhoea sound-effects made by squeezing custard-filled balloon into a bucket.

21

SKIVING OFF HOME EARLY.

One of the best excuses for knocking off halfway through the afternoon is to invent a sudden emergency at home - the more awful, tragic and heart-rending the better.

IT'S THE FIRE BRIGADE... MY CAT HAS EXPLODED!!

I CAN FINISH THAT PAPERWORK FIRST IF YOU WANT ME TO...

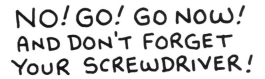

NO! GO! GO NOW! AND DON'T FORGET YOUR SCREWDRIVER!

BEEP! BEEP!

I've also found it useful in the past, if I wanted to skive off from the office, to let the boss think I was a part-time member of a special Territorial Army bomb disposal unit that would only be called out if there was a local emergency involving terrorists planting a nuclear device in the area.

You might also like to try this. Apart from being guaranteed to get you out of the office faster than greased lightning, it's worth it just to see the look on your boss's face when your "top secret Territorial Army nuclear bomb warning bleeper" goes off halfway through a quiet Friday afternoon.

COMING IN LATE.

If, in addition to skiving off early, you also make a habit of coming in late in the morning, you can really shave some serious time off the unreasonably long and exhausting hours that many bosses expect you to work.

But of course you run the risk that your boss will notice your repeated late arrivals and start lying in wait to catch you with a notice of dismissal clutched in his sweaty mitt.

A good disguise is the best answer; e.g. postman, motorcycle messenger, aged tea-trolley lady, gorilla (bosses tend to be a bit dim and easily fooled).

Over the years I built up a collection of disguises for sneaking in past waiting bosses so vast and ingenious, Inspector Clousseau himself would be impressed.

Office pot-plant disguise (move very, very, very, very slowly past waiting boss, inching your way along office wall each time he looks down to glance at his watch).

23

HAVING FUN IN THE OFFICE

OFFICE GAMES AND PASTIMES.

Of course these days playing computer games is one of the most popular office pastimes (when the boss isn't looking).

But I'm also a great fan of the more traditional low-tech games and pastimes that have provided generations of office workers with much-needed moments of light relief to break up the monotony of daily office routine. Like making paper airplanes and flicking rubber bands; essential office skills throughout the ages and just as valuable today.

For maximum entertainment value and general office moral-boosting effect, choose a target and devise a suitable points system so everyone can join in and compete for the highest score.

Boss's bald head: 10 points.

Extra 5 points for trick shots.

Boss's nose: 15 points.

Boss's coffee cup: 15 points.

Boss's bum: 5 points.

PING!

FLICK!

PING!

A mini basketball hoop or mini darts board that you can stick on the office wall near your desk is another excellent idea to help you while away those boring bits of office life in between coffee breaks, lunch and going home.

If you don't have a wall near your desk on which to hang a hoop or darts board, don't worry; with a wire coat hanger, some glue or tape, and a motorbike or cycle crash helmet you can quickly construct something on these lines.

Simply persuade a nearby co-worker (preferably a rather dim and easily persuaded one) to wear it, and you're away.

Even if you <u>do</u> have a wall near your desk, you may still prefer to utilise the "Office Games Helmet" (®™) anyway, since a moving target is always more of a challenge (not to mention the added amusement value of annoying the hell out of the sort of wimpy, soft co-worker who's daft enough to agree to something like that).

25

MAKING AN OFFICE CALENDAR.

This can be great fun and very easy, since
so many offices now have quite sophisticated
desk-top publishing capabilities which,
combined with a digital camera, make
producing your own office calendar,
using your own photos, so simple.

HAVING FUN ON THE PHONE.

This can be a great laugh but is also a good way to cope with a busy phone day in the office; the kind of day when you just can't get on with those important tasks like finishing your crossword puzzle because the bloody phone won't stop ringing.

For example, you'll be surprised just how quickly callers will hang up if they think they're talking not to someone in an office but to a fiendishly complicated and incomprehensible automated answering service, are waiting in a queue, have to listen to brain-rottingly bad 'on hold' music, or think they've got through to an incredibly inappropriate wrong number.

IF YOUR ENQUIRY WILL BE LESS THAN FIVE WORDS, PRESS ONE... IF IT WILL BE MORE THAN A HUNDRED WORDS, PRESS TWO... IF YOU WANT TO SPEAK IN A DEEP VOICE, PRESS THREE... IF YOU...

FORGET IT !!

WELCOME TO "QUICKIE-CUM"! THIS CALL WILL APPEAR ON YOUR PHONE BILL AS A LIVE SEX CHAT....

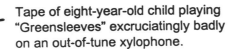

Tape of eight-year-old child playing "Greensleeves" excruciatingly badly on an out-of-tune xylophone.

27

COPING WITH PAPERWORK.

If you find your paperwork is always piling up and your boss just keeps dumping more on you, here is a neat and simple procedure that should solve your problem.

WHIRRR!

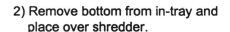

1) Cut hole in desk-top and insert paper shredding machine.

2) Remove bottom from in-tray and place over shredder.

3) Switch on shredder and sit back.

Remove and bin shredded paperwork when desk drawers start to fill up and you can't find your chocolate biscuits.

COPING WITH COMPUTER PROBLEMS.

What can I say? We all know what's <u>really</u> going on with computers, but the reality is just too horrifying to contemplate. Instead we fart around with maddeningly incomprehensible manuals and useless 'Help' menus.

THE OFFICE WHIP-ROUND.

As everyone knows, this can be a real pain in the arse; having to constantly put your hand in your pocket for people you hardly know just because they're retiring after a hundred years with the firm, taking maternity leave to have quintuplets, getting married again, or having yet another bloody birthday!

Personally, over the years I've found the best answer is to always offer to take the collecting tin around and buy the present.

That way you can laugh your socks off as you drink away the proceeds in your favourite pub, while old Albert from accounting wonders why, after forty-eight years of loyal service, all he got as a leaving present was a pencil with a rubber tip shaped like Snoopy.

KEEPING FIT IN THE OFFICE.

The sedentary office lifestyle, sitting around on your bum all the time munching chocolate biscuits and drinking coffee, can pose some serious health risks.

I recommend that you find time to fit some simple and easy office-based exercise routines into your day. Here is my basic office work-out, which has kept me fit and health for years (video available soon, price £15-99p plus P&P):

1) Do this vigorously and repeatedly behind boss's back at least 50 times a day, using alternate hands.

2) At least 10 times a day sneak up behind boss and pretend to kick him up the bum over and over again.

3) Combine 1) and 2) with a preliminary run, skip, hop and jump across the office for a full aerobic work-out.